Pets
AROUND
the WORLD

by Brenna Maloney

Children's Press®
An imprint of Scholastic Inc.

Library of Congress Cataloging-in-Publication Data
Names: Maloney, Brenna, author.
Title: Pets around the world/Brenna Maloney.
Description: First edition. | New York: Children's Press, an imprint of Scholastic Inc., 2021. |
   Series: Around the world | Includes index. | Audience: Ages 5–7. | Audience: Grades K–1. |
   Summary: "This book shows young readers some of the many ways people take care of
   their pets around the world"— Provided by publisher.
Identifiers: LCCN 2021000138 (print) | LCCN 2021000139 (ebook) | ISBN 9781338768732 (library binding) |
   ISBN 9781338768749 (paperback) | ISBN 9781338768756 (ebook)
Subjects: LCSH: Pets—Juvenile literature. | Pets—Cross-cultural studies—Juvenile literature.
Classification: LCC SF416.2 .M255 2021 (print) | LCC SF416.2 (ebook) | DDC 636.088/7—dc23
LC record available at https://lccn.loc.gov/2021000138
LC ebook record available at https://lccn.loc.gov/2021000139

10 9 8 7 6 5 4 3 2 1   22 23 24 25 26

Printed in Heshan, China 62
First edition, 2022

Series produced by Spooky Cheetah Press
Cover and book design by Kimberly Shake

Photos ©: cover top left, 1 top left: real444/Getty Images; cover top right, 1 top right: Peopleimages/Getty Images; cover bottom right, 1 bottom right: Margot Hartford/age fotostock; 3: Kashin Sergey Alekseevich/Getty Images; 4 left: Creatas/Getty Images; 4 center: Westend61/Getty Images; 4 right: Ryan McVay/Getty Images; 5 left: imageBROKER/Shutterstock; 5 right: Muriel de Seze/Getty Images; 7: BraunS/Getty Images; 9: Ross Brown/EyeEm/Getty Images; 10: Anne-Sophie Bost/age fotostock; 11: J.-M. Labat & F. Rouquette/Biosphoto; 14: Charli Bandit/Getty Images; 17: Trinity Mirror/Mirrorpix/Alamy Images; 19: Fuse/Getty Images; 20: Justice/Getty Images; 22: Carlo Allegri/Getty Images; 23: lucidwaters/age fotostock; 25: Cris Bouroncle/AFP/Getty Images; 26-27 background: Jim McMahon/Mapman ®; 26 top: M_a_y_a/Getty Images; 27 bottom right: Behrouz Mehri/AFP/Getty Images; 28 left: Kim Hong-Ji/Reuters/Newscom; 28 center: Lucio Virzi/Flickr; 29 top: Emily Bruno/FarmetteKitchen.com; 29 bottom left: Vyacheslav Madiyevskyy/Avalon.red/Newscom; 29 bottom center: Francois Guillot/AFP/Getty Images; 29 bottom right: Carolyn Snowden/Jacksonville Dog Cafe; 31: Jaap Schelvis/Buitenbeeld/Minden Pictures.

All other photos © Shutterstock.

TABLE of CONTENTS

JUST LIKE ME

Kids in every country around the world have a lot in common. They go to school and play. They have families and friends. Still, some things—like their pets—can be very different!

SPAIN

ENGLAND

UNITED STATES

Can an alpaca
be a family
pet? You bet!

FRANCE

PERU

5

chapter 1

OUR BEST FRIENDS

More than half of the people in the world have pets. Dogs, cats, fish, and birds are the most popular. In the United States, pups are tops. There is nearly one dog for every four Americans. India has one of the fastest-growing dog **populations** in the world.

Beagles are one of the most popular types of dogs in India.

Many people in the United States have Labrador retrievers as pets.

The shih tzu is a small dog that is popular in Brazil.

Some people like smaller pups. There are more small dogs in Brazil than in any other country. Big dogs, such as salukis, are the favorite in Saudi Arabia. About 70 percent of the pet dogs in that country are large **breeds**.

The saluki is also known as the Arabian hound.

The world has slightly fewer pet cats than pet dogs. But cat owners often have more than one cat at a time. Russian blue cats are very popular in Russia. Some people think they bring good luck. Rome, Italy, is home to a lot of **stray** cats. People feed the cats and look after them.

Russian blues are very playful cats!

In Italy, strays are called "free cats."

11

Home aquariums are popular in Turkey.

12

chapter 2
FINS AND FEATHERS

They are quiet and colorful. And they never need to be walked! No wonder fish are such popular pets. That is especially true in France, where there is an average of eight fish per household. Pet owners in Turkey also love fish. That country is home to the world's largest tunnel **aquarium**.

Visitors to the Antalya Aquarium in Turkey can see more than 1,500 **species** of fish!

Parrots, doves, and parakeets—these birds are common pets around the world. But did you know that chickens can be pets, too? In England, chickens are a favorite choice. The most popular pet bird in Egypt is the pigeon. Pigeons are known to be gentle pets.

Pigeons may be the first birds to have been kept as pets.

Chickens can be trained to do tricks!

15

chapter 3

FUR AND SCALES

Belgium is the place for rabbits—especially large ones! That is where the Flemish giant is found. This bunny really lives up to its name! In Chile, chinchillas are more popular than rabbits. These cuddly creatures have supersoft fur and are very smart.

Chinchillas are **native** to South America.

Flemish giants can weigh up to 22 pounds (10 kilograms)!

Tortoises can live for 50 years or more!

Reptiles are popular pets around the world. Some people keep lizards, snakes, and turtles. In Taiwan, tortoises are treasured. They don't take up much space. That makes them a good choice for people who live in apartments. In Spain, pet owners favor iguanas and snakes.

Iguanas eat plants. They like dark leafy greens such as kale.

chapter 4
UNCOMMON COMPANIONS

Insects don't often top the list of popular pets. But crickets are a favorite pet in China. People love the beautiful music they make. In Japan, beetles are a top pet. They are small, quiet, and easy to keep. Some Japanese pet stores sell only beetles and beetle supplies.

In China, crickets are often kept in fancy cages.

Rhinoceros beetles (pictured) and stag beetles are popular pets in Japan.

Wild animals aren't usually pets. But in some parts of Australia, wallabies may become part of a family. Caregivers sometimes help out when a wild animal is injured or **orphaned**. One man in Canada adopted an orphaned baby bison that grew to weigh almost 1,600 pounds (725 kilograms). Now, that's a big pet!

This bison's name was Bailey D. Buffalo. He lived in Canada.

Wallabies are found in Australia and on nearby islands.

Alpacas are originally from Peru. But now they are found throughout South America.

24

Sometimes a farm animal can also be a pet. That is the case with alpacas in Peru. People sell their pet alpacas' soft **fleece** in markets.

You have learned about a lot of different pets—from Labradors to lizards. What is your favorite type of pet?

Alpaca fleece is made into soft yarn for clothing.

IF YOU LIVED HERE . . .

Let's learn more about different pets around the world!

UNITED STATES
About 3.2 million dogs and cats are adopted from shelters every year.

BRAZIL
Some people in Brazil keep capybaras as pets. They are the world's largest rodents!

NORWAY

People here spend more on dog food every month than in any other country in the world.

JAPAN

Some pets in this country are really pampered! Special treats include designer outfits, nail painting, and spa treatments.

SPAIN

More than 20 million pets live here. That's a lot more than the number of kids under the age of 15.

A CLOSER LOOK

People who don't have pets can visit
pet cafés around the world.

South Korea

Visitors can eat banana-strawberry waffles in the company of fluffy sheep at the Thanks Nature Cafe in Seoul.

Italy

Rome's Romeow Cat Bistrot gives people a break from a busy day. Visitors can enjoy a healthy snack with the resident cats.

Thailand

Siberian huskies bring the love at the TrueLove Café in Bangkok. After guests eat, they can play with and feed ice chips to these fluffy dogs.

Visitors to the Thanks Nature Cafe in South Korea can enjoy sheep-themed desserts!

Ukraine

The Raccoon Café in Kharkiv specializes in more than coffee! There is a separate room where visitors can play with or pet raccoons.

France

A visit to Le Café des Chats in Paris can include sinking into cozy armchairs, enjoying delicious treats, and playing with friendly cats.

United States

Visitors to the Jacksonville Dog Cafe in Florida can cuddle a pup while sipping coffee—and maybe meet a forever friend. These dogs can be adopted!

GLOSSARY

aquarium (uh-KWAIR-ee-uhm) a place set up for visitors to see different kinds of water-dwelling creatures

breeds (BREEDZ) particular types of plants or animals

fleece (FLEES) the woolly coat of a sheep, an alpaca, or a similar animal

native (NAY-tiv) living or growing naturally in a certain place

orphaned (OR-fuhnd) (of an animal) without a living mother

populations (pahp-yuh-LAY-shuhnz) the total number of living things in a place

rodents (ROH-duhntz) small mammals, such as rats and squirrels, with large, sharp front teeth used for gnawing

shelters (SHEL-turz) places where animals that have no homes can stay and be cared for

species (SPEE-sheez) one of the groups into which animals and plants are divided

stray (STRAY) lost or having no home

31

INDEX

ABOUT THE AUTHOR

Brenna Maloney is a writer and an editor. She has had many pets, including cats, dogs, guinea pigs, hamsters, rabbits, gerbils, birds, fish, bees, and even Madagascar hissing cockroaches.